I0108814

The Schools of the
Scottish Episcopal Church

THE SCHOOLS

OF THE

Scottish Episcopal Church.

No. I.

ABERDEEN: A. BROWN & CO.
EDINBURGH: R. GRANT & SON.
LONDON: LONGMAN & CO.
1870.

3d.

THE SCHOOLS

SCOTTISH EPISCOPAL CHURCH.

No. I.

THE friends of our Church Schools are not altogether without cause alarmed as to the present movement of the Equal Dividend. It is well that there should be a clear understanding as to what is aimed at. It is very desirable to my mind that the Clergy and School Funds should be entirely distinct—that each fund should be raised upon its own merits.

Providing a decent maintenance for her Clergy is the first duty of a Church, and removing the present scandal that rests upon us is undoubtedly the great work before us, for neglect of the Clergy implies want of spiritual development in the Church. But it by no means follows that we are to neglect the teaching of the young. Teaching the young in the principles of the Church cannot be neglected without inflicting upon herself vital injury. A very cursory retrospect of the history of our Church must convince any one that until our Church took up the School question she made no solid advance in the country. The Schools indeed have been the most successful part of our Church's operations, and have reaped the largest fruit. The very fact of the probability of a secular system being established in Scotland should stimulate us to renewed exertions in this respect, for the simple reason that secular schools really mean the teaching the principles of the religion of the preponderating creed of the country. The secular principle has been discarded in England; even if carried in Scotland it will be evaded in its working. So far from suspending all exertions in the way of education, it appears to me at no time were the friends of the Church called upon to make greater exertions than at present in this department. It is therefore that I advocate our giving to the Church with reference to the Schools upon their own merits. The more earnest we show ourselves in the work the more likely we are to have good terms from the Government, and what especially appears to me to commend itself to our support is the Training Institution. It is specially necessary that teachers should be provided who understand our wants and the feelings of the country. Englishmen, as a rule, can only acquire this after long experience; and it is most desirable that an indigenous class should be maintained for the supply of the increasing wants of the Church. In fact our Church is bound, were it only for her own preservation, to carry on the policy she is committed to, viz., to spread her schools over the breadth and length of the country;

and the time has now arrived that she should take a
· decided line as to future measures that may be intro-
duced into Parliament. The spirit and character of
them may be easily conjectured; and it is only
through want of preparation upon our part that any
measure will be carried injurious to the interests of
our Church. The present machinery of our Government only admits of one class taking the matter up,
but still the laity can meet the Clergy in public meeting and discuss the matter in full. Even the Synods
can be convened with lay representatives present, and
an aggregate committee appointed to deal with the
whole question; for should a general system of education be established, of a Presbyterian character, it is
clear that our religious system will have to contend
with the greatest difficulties; and it is only by the
preservation of our schools that our members can be
retained to the Church.

With regard to the much vaunted secular system,
the instances in which it is conducted are in no way
favourable to the continuance of the system. At the
beginning, the ministers of the various denominations
may supervise the education of the members of their
systems, but it seems improbable that this supervision
can long be continued. It forms no part of the system
of the schools; and is a supererogatory act altogether.
The consequence is there is practically no religious
teaching at all, and should this be spread over the
country, we shall soon drift into a German Canton.
The laity have quite as much a direct interest in this
matter as the Clergy, for independently of their ulti-
mate prospects as to taking a part in the government

of the Church, we have quite enough to contend with
in the way of a majority of the country, without going
out of our way to debar any children from the means
of education in the principles of our Church. The
notion that our Church would acquire an advantage
from the schools of the country being thrown over to
the competition of the sects, is one of those Utopian
dreams that never has been realised. The object of
teaching is not to minimise religion; it is to make the
most of it. We must present, then, an united front
upon this matter to Parliament and to the country;
and whilst anxious to throw no obstacles in the way
of a measure for the education of the people, we are
not in any way prepared to sacrifice our schools,
which must necessarily ever be the mainstay of the
Church of Christ. This is a matter, then, that the
laity should make up their minds to deal with. Any
hesitation upon this matter at the present crisis may
lead to consequences which cannot afterwards be re-
paired. Large districts of the country are open to
evangelization by our Church, which, under the present system of government in our Church, must
remain unbroken. The great mass of our poor must
remain undealt with until the resources of the Church
can be rightly developed, through renewed life in the
Church herself. Government by a class necessarily
throws all the work upon the class which rules, and
renders that class alone interested in what is being
done. Hence the system of our schools, and indeed
of every other department in our Church may be said
to be still in its infancy. We are but groping about
and availing ourselves of such means as Providence has

supplied us with. The laity are still a class without the system ; and until they be resuscitated as a class, it is not reasonable to expect that our Church can make much advance, nor is it to be expected that a class long dead to the Church can be mesmerised into continuous life, until the resuscitation be complete. The working of the Church is necessarily slow. The spiritual life of all of us is a continuous struggle beset by constant failures. The ways of the Church essentially differ from those of the world, for the individual soul makes progress by failures. The man of the world makes progress by success. To wean back to the Church a class long ostracised is then a tedious process ; and it would not be healthy were it otherwise in its operation, for the laity to be useful in the Church must he weaned from the world. To infuse spiritual life into the laity—to separate them from the world and its ways—to educate them into a due sense of the privileges of the " Priesthood " of which they are members—such a work is the great work of the Church, for without accomplishing all this the Church herself must ever be *dead*. The dead weight of a laity—immersed in the attaining of worldly honour and living " for the world "—must necessarily demoralise all around it—most paralyse all the efforts of the Church—must arrest its progress—and reflect a false glare upon apparent victories. It is like gaining converts, because our Church is so aristocratic, or because our Church is in communion with the Church of England. The secularity which pervades our Church necessarily shuts men's eyes to the advantages of " schools," and to their future developments—missions.

This question of Schools then involves questions affecting the vital interests of the Church, for it strikes at what necessarily forms and constitutes the spiritual life of the Church. Without this the Church may preserve an exterior of prosperity, and may even gain the respect of the world, but the system cannot last. It has no basis for permanence, for it deceives itself. No gorgeousness of architecture, and no eloquence of preaching can compensate for what is in itself hollow and delusive. It has got out of the track, and there is no chart by which it can return or be guided, unless that fixed by the Catholic Church of all ages—Schools and Missions. Schools are the pioneers of the spiritual development of the Church, and without them all is dead. I myself entertain no fears as to the results of the present struggle, for Schools and Missions are valuable as tests of the spiritual progress of the Church. A Church may for a time, as indeed, alas! an individual soul may, go backwards. It may preserve a lingering existence and die away. But such are not the signs of our times. Contrasting the Church of 1870 with that of 1852, a small minority, interested in the Church, have swelled into a large majority. Things denounced then as Utopian and visionary have become accomplished facts. The progress of opinion has been as unconscious as it has been certain. The movement has worked itself out, certainly not on account of any skill in its management, but rather from its blunders, because " it was of God." To suppose, then, that our Church, at this time of day, is " to go backwards," is to contradict all the phenomena around us. But as it is in the case of the individual soul, so it is in the Church; it is at the time when we imagine we are most secure that we really are in the greatest danger. It is amidst affliction and misfortune that the individual soul is brought nearer to God. As a rule, men think more of eternity when "going backward" in the world than upward. So it is with the Church as a body; and we trust that she will not be misled by her onward progress, but still rather meditate upon the breakers ahead. In retiring from a position which she at present occupies in advance, in proportion to her numbers, of every body of Christians in Scotland, she will stultify herself before the country, and undo, so far as she can, the progress made within a quarter of a century. The fact of there being no great immediate results is really no argument against the system. It is not desirable the Church should meet with spasmodic success, nor does she profess to do so. It is in this again the work of the Church differs from that of the world, for success is really no criterion whereby to judge, for error as a rule more nearly accords with the tendencies of the human heart. What is in itself popular, necessarily belongs more to the world than the Church. The fact of the Missions move in 1866 not producing larger results than it did, is really no argument against it, for it showed the Church was not prepared for it. To engage in Missions at all argues a certain amount of spiritual development amongst the members of the Church, and so far from acting as any reason for giving up the original scheme, is rather an argument the other way. So soon as the Synods represent fairly the Church, so soon must that scheme be taken up and dealt with, whether through diocesan or general action, for it is a work which the Church must undertake sooner or later. The practical exclusion of the poor from her services is indefensible as a rule upon every principle of the Catholic Church, which professes to be essentially the Church of the Poor; and until our Church takes up her right position in this matter, she cannot expect to, nor is it desirable that she should, make much advance in Scotland. In the meantime we must make the most of what we have got. It is not by throwing up their arms that soldiers gain a battle. It is not by throwing over the teaching of her children in the principles of the Church that the Church can either benefit herself or gain the respect of the community. It might be a " popular " act, but it would be like most " popular " acts, singularly unwise. It is not by constant changes of opinion that individuals or bodies inspire confidence. It is by a consistent line of policy, intelligible to all round, that great victories are ultimately achieved.

I should then urge upon Churchmen to go to the country with regard to the Schools upon their own merits. It is possible that the response may not be what it should be. It is therefore the more desirable that the question should be widely agitated—that every pulpit should resound with the cry, " Maintain the Schools !" It would be quite as mischievous to mix up the question of the Equal Dividend with the question of the Schools for the Clergy, as for the cause of education. No blessing could be conferred upon a movement which made the interests of the Clergy clash with the first elements of spiritual life in the

Church, for no money could repay the injury inflicted. It would ultimately turn the tide of public opinion, which has at present its full sympathies, against the Stipends question, and would raise a different platform upon a very equivocal issue, to say the least of it ; so, in advocating the Equal Dividend, I hope it will be clearly understood that we do not consider that the Equal Dividend in any way relates to the Schools. The Equal Dividend stands upon its own merits. People understand what they are subscribing to when they do so. They equally understand what they are doing when they subscribe to the Schools. The issues can co-operate, but there is no use of mixing them up. Both important in their separate branches, they form an essential element of all Church Finance ; and we trust that the Church will bestow that careful and discriminating attention upon these two issues, essential to a right adjustment of such important questions. No greater blunder can be made in Church Finance than that one scheme militates against another. The doctrine that it is dangerous having too many irons in the fire is a complete fallacy, for the more schemes in operation, the more the Church engages the sympathies of different classes of opinion. A Church only thrives by constant movement, so long as that movement is healthy, temperate, and defined. A Church must move forward like each individual member in the Church, for the Church is a mere aggregation of individual souls, and upon each individual executing his work in the Church depends the prosperity of the Church. This movement must be regulated by recognised authority, and must be in conformity to the will of the Church. The two questions now before the Church —the question of the Stipends and the question of the Schools—are questions that cannot be ignored. They embody the common sense of the Church. The neglect of them involves wilful tampering with first duties to the Church. To awaken the public conscience to these duties is the business of every member—one member can influence a family, another can influence a congregation ; a combination of men can influence a diocese. I may be told this is "the old story." The fact of this being an old story does not weaken the argument ; it makes it all the stronger. First duties are generally those the most neglected. The human heart recoils from the drudgery of life. It seeks after some novelty to escape fulfilling plain and primary obligations. There is no escaping from the issues raised ; and the fact of want of success in previous experiments furnishes no argument against persevering in the wish : continue our Clergy in their present pecuniary position—diminish the schools. What next ? When once the Church goes downhill, what can arrest the descent ? The faith of her children can re-construct the whole system of our Church, can repair past defeats, can place her financial system upon a solid basis. Even though defeat follow the present efforts, the agitation must be continued. The agitation must act as the beating of the water against a rock, which in the course of ages gives way to the continuous shock. Whether successful or not, we must go on. The establishment of the Equal Dividend will raise an intelligible issue before the country, and will besides place the Clergy upon a more independent footing than they yet have occupied. It will emancipate them from congregational control, and will excite the interests and feelings of Churchmen in a common cause. The Schools will equally appeal to the first feelings of all parents of families— the education of the young. Upon the settlement of these two great questions hangs the whole future of our Church.

The Church ever adapts herself to the incidents of her position. Whether under the exclusive rule of Bishops, or else of Bishop and Presbyter, the work is the same—the saving of souls. Beset as all works here below are by human infirmity and human error, the work must be executed. One generation succeeds another in rapid succession, and each has its office and its mission. No defects in government can atone for neglect in the performance of the work. However clumsy or however skilful our performance, the account must be rendered as to how we have performed the work. Failure or success makes little difference, so long as the work is done.

HUGH SCOTT
OF GALA.

MADEIRA, *November*, 1870.

ABERDEEN:
PRINTED BY ARTHUR KING AND COMPANY, STEAM PRINTERS AND STEREOTYPERS,
CLARK'S COURT, TOP OF BROAD STREET.

By the same Author.

THE POSITION OF THE LAITY

IN THE

SCOTTISH EPISCOPAL CHURCH.

Nos. 1, 2, 3, 4, & 5.

PRICE 3d. EACH.

THE

FINANCIAL PROSPECTS

OF THE

Scottish Episcopal Church.

Nos. 1 2, & 3.

PRICE 3d. EACH.

ABERDEEN: A. BROWN & CO.

The Schools of the
Scottish Episcopal Chur

No 2

THE SCHOOLS

OF THE

Scottish Episcopal Church.

No. II.

ABERDEEN:
A. BROWN & CO.
EDINBURGH: R. GRANT & SON.
LONDON: LONGMAN & CO.
1870.

3d.

ABERDEEN:

PRINTED BY ARTHUR KING AND COMPANY, STEAM PRINTERS AND STEREOTYPERS,

CLARKS. COURT, TOP OF BROAD STREET.

THE SCHOOLS

SCOTTISH EPISCOPAL CHURCH.

No. II.

THE warm response which I have received from all
parts of the Church, with reference to the question of
the Schools, induces me to believe that the Church
will move as a whole, and will present an united front
upon a matter affecting her vital interests as a Church.
The maintenance of our Training Institution and our
Schools appears so obvious a duty, that it appears
very much like saying that two and two make four;
and it is precisely because it is so axiomatic that it is
all the more likely to be neglected; and I trust that
the friends of our Schools will not be lulled into a false
security, but will carry on a continuous agitation upon
this question, whether in the form of Petitions to Parliament or ventilating the matter at Meetings of the
Congregations, so that the mind of the Church may be
clearly ascertained, and a clear line of policy determined on. The Primus has, in a speech at Aberdeen,

sent a warning note through the Church, and it would only spoil the case to make any addenda to the matter; but irrespectively of the opinions of those with whom we are most nearly associated in matters of policy, those most opposed to us in all our schemes for the last twenty years, who view all signs of progress in our Church with alarm, are on this matter at any rate our most strenuous supporters. The opinion seems all but universal throughout the Church (and the most reactionary are, singular to say, by some peculiar inconsistency not capable of explanation, the most alive to the danger), that the Church must now speak, not through the Bishops, nor even through a committee of a society, but in its every part, and take a determinate line intelligible to the country and the Government, and resist any renewal of the efforts made two years ago to Presbyterianise her Schools, and violate all the engagements to which Parliament has committed the Privy Council. We have, besides all this, the notorious fact before us, that Mr. Gladstone, of all men, is committed more than any other man to those solemn engagements, and that no cabinet can compel him to a violation of these engagements such as the bill of the Duke of Argyle so outrageously set at nought. We ask no favour. We simply demand justice. Our Schools are built under distinct engagements, and to these engagements we adhere. The State cannot throw us off without committing a manifest breach of public faith. Churchmen in England have been very fond of giving us advice—of endeavouring to convince us that they understand the management of our affairs a good deal better than we do ourselves—a great opportunity is now before them of manifesting their good-will by saving our Schools from the threatened ruin. It is no use repeating their advice through their "special correspondents," unless they render active aid in a matter affecting the very existence of our Church. We have a clear claim upon them as members of the Catholic Church to render us assistance in this, for it is difficult to see, if they do not help us in this, what we can hereafter expect them to help us in. It will be very much like asking our friends to extinguish flames in our house after the house has been burnt down. We have a claim upon the Clergy in especial. No class in the Church have a greater experience of the necessity of Schools ; no class are more aware of the disastrous consequences attending the policy of putting our Schools at the mercy of the sects ; no class have been louder in denouncing the fallacy, that the Schools interfered with their stipends, for no class were better aware of the plain common sense, that anything that reduced the number of the congregations necessarily brought down the stipends. The Executive Committee of the Church Society, if recognised by the Church, will doubtless exercise a wise discretion in the management of the movement. It is true that it is a matter with which they really have nothing to do, but in the present provisional state of our Church's constitution we must make the best of what we have got ; and I trust the Laity will make no scruple as to any informality in their constitution. At the same time, I trust that each diocese will move in its separate sphere, and will regulate the agitation through the different congregations. Should the Bishops not deem fit to convoke the Diocesan Synods, the laity at any rate can meet amongst themselves, and can petition, can assemble in public meeting, and can influence their representatives in Parliament. That the Duke of Argyle was quite unconscious of the mischief he was doing I fully believe. We could not expect him to show us much consideration, but so soon as he understands the grievous wrong he was inflicting upon us, and so soon as he sees we are determined to assert our rights, as well as realise the importance of the country adhering to its engagements, we have every reason to believe that such concession will be made as will retain inviolate existing rights, if not render that tardy justice which later legislation has in some measure meted out to us. At any rate Penal Laws have not stamped us out as yet; and it is not likely that a re-enactment of any Penal Act will now-a-days accomplish its purpose. Under any circumstances, I trust that the bulk of the work will not be thrown upon the Bishops. Even though without the pale of the Constitution, the Laity have quite as much interest in the Church as their Lordships or any other class; and we are quite as capable of forming a right judgment upon this matter as any other class in the Church, and are much more likely to render as effectual resistance to this aggression upon our rights. Let there then be no squeamishness about acting freely and speaking our mind very plainly about the matter, and let us at once get rid of the notion that the Laity have nothing to do with Church affairs, and that the Church is maintained simply for the aggrandisement of a class. We indeed in no way undervalue the co-operation of our Spiritual Fathers, but what we do feel is this, that too much work is continually being thrown upon them in Church affairs; and that by a fair division of work the Church would be more largely represented and the work better done.

The present time is, however, no time for stirring up class questions, for we are now struggling for bare existence. This is, it is true, nothing new. Penal Laws have done their best to stamp us out, and it remains to be seen, whether in this so-called age of progress, a fresh attempt will be made to revive a penal enactment. It can only be by our own listlessness that this can be accomplished. We have as yet made a wonderful escape, and should take warning from the fact. A wise Providence has hitherto protected us from a complete sweep of our Schools so far as legislation could do it. Providence as a rule only helps those who help themselves, and it can only be by showing to the country and Parliament that we are prepared to fight every clause of the bill that infringes upon our hard-earned rights. If the Government is to go in for penal legislation, let it say so ; but do not let it throw dust in the eyes of the country, and under cover of a Bill, for establishing a system of education for the whole country, in which religion is expunged nominally, in reality establish Schools under an enforced assessment, for the propagandism of one creed. Let not Government delude themselves by supposing that Scotland will ever tolerate a godless system. It is opposed to the whole feelings and traditions of the country, and no Act of Parliament can enforce it. It has been found unworkable in Ireland. It has been given up in England. Why try the experiment in Scotland ? the country most opposed both by historic memories and national feelings, to the experiment.

Whilst doing all this, the agitation for the recovery of Lay Rights must be actively continued. The very question of the Schools manifests the evil of class government, for the inaction that prevails amongst the Laity upon this matter arises from the fact of their exclusion from all part in the government of the Church, and any weakness that may be shown in the front we present to the Government upon this matter, will be caused by the long-established inertia of a class deprived of all life by legislation. The School question is the most pressing; for confiscation of our property is actually threatened, and may rouse the Laity to a sense of the duty they owe to the Church; but there are equally important questions hanging over which must be sooner or later dealt with, and cannot be much longer postponed without doing serious detriment to the best interests of the Church.

Whilst the Schools' question is dealt with by the Church at large through congregational, diocesan, and aggregate committees, let the lay agitation go on with revived vigour. We hold a vantage ground in 1871 we have never occupied before. The whole of the Diocesan Synods have pronounced in favour of the principle, and have petitioned the College of Bishops to convene a General Synod for the adjustment of the lay question. The College of Bishops are, by the resolution of 1852, committed to the principle. We are bound to support the Synods in their petition, more especially when several of the Bishops have represented to the country that we have changed our minds upon the matter, and that upon this ground they have resisted the mind of the whole Church. We are bound, in justice to ourselves, to prove to the College of Bishops that their information is erroneous by numerously signed petitions, and by a more organised system of agitation than as yet has been attempted. There are periods in the histories of nations, of churches, and of individuals, when boldness is true wisdom. We cannot now go back even if we wished it. Public opinion has borne us along, and will go on itself in spite of us. The whole Anglican communion is shaken to its very centre upon this question, and upon a right solution of it hangs our whole future. The two movements can go on hand in hand, and can help each other, for the more the Laity are interested in the Church, and the more they are occupied in agitating for their rights, the more certainly they will be deeply concerned in the matter of the Schools. The fact of being interested in one department of the Church's affairs necessarily interests one in all its concerns. As to whether the Bishops will accede to the wishes of the Laity and the whole Church is a different question. The formation of a healthy public opinion—the education of the popular mind —the ventilation of the whole question in the press and social circles—all this is the Laity's work. All great popular triumphs have been accomplished by the struggles and efforts of the class concerned. We are bound to show every respect and deference to our Spiritual Fathers, but we are bound at the same time to speak our own mind very freely upon a question we are most concerned in. Any violent language or hasty action can only damage the cause affected, but what we are bound to do in justice to ourselves is to prove to the Bishops and the country that we are in earnest—that we shall proceed calmly, deliberately, and resolutely, in the work before us—that no reverses will daunt us—that we stand upon the platform they themselves erected in 1852—and that there will be no pause, no cessation in the agitation, until we regain our rights in full. If we are in a minority on the question there is the more reason for agitation. The sooner we become a majority the better; and it is certain we can do no good by sitting with our hands before us. The question is one raised by the Bishops themselves, and it is a question, the settlement of which cannot be postponed without inflicting serious detriment upon the Church.

In the mean time the Schools' question is the one which presses most upon us. It must be taken up in earnest by the Church, and the machinery for an agitation of the question must be organised without delay. Let the members of the Church but do their duty, and there can be but one issue to the contest. Let her for once act with decision, and give up that temporising policy which has so painfully distinguished her in the eyes of Christendom for the last twenty years, and look the thing fairly in the face. Let us at once proclaim to the country that the matter will be fought out, and let the Churchmen in England understand this. The true reason why Churchmen in England take little or no interest in our concerns, is from the policy of our Church not having been consistent in itself, nor intelligible to ourselves. The policy of conciliation, as it has been called, has created distrust amongst our friends, without insuring the good-will of our opponents.

The Schools' question presents a platform upon which all sections of the Church can meet, and *now is the time* if we are to move at all. If we do not, we must make up our minds at once to a public confiscation, under the name of an assessment for the benefit of the Presbyterian creed. All this can be averted if we show confidence in ourselves and in our Church. The voice of faction must be hushed in the midst of the combat, for the combat is, without the smallest disguise, for the very existence of our Church. Whatever others may do, so far as we are concerned, the battle will be fought out, and we entertain little or no doubt as to the issue of the fight.

HUGH SCOTT,
OF GALA.

MADEIRA, *January,* 1871.

THE SCHOOLS

Scottish Episcopal Church.

No. III.

ABERDEEN:

A. BROWN & CO.

EDINBURGH: R. GRANT & SON.

LONDON: LONGMANS & CO.

1871.

3d.

ABERDEEN:
PRINTED BY ARTHUR KING AND COMPANY, STEAM PRINTERS AND STEREOTYPERS
CLARK'S COURT, TOP OF BROAD STREET.

THE SCHOOLS

OF THE

SCOTTISH EPISCOPAL CHURCH.

No. III.

THE late victory which we have gained in the matter of the Schools must not blind us to the dangers still impending over us. It was gratifying to observe the very general response our last appeal met with from the Church ; and the numerous petitions presented to Parliament demonstrated a zeal and intelligent interest in the cause of education, for which previous experiences had not prepared me. The late charges of the Primus and the Bishop of St. Andrews deal with the question in its present position as one of compromise. The compromise they propose, though better than nothing, and worthy of all attention, will yet revolutionize the whole system of our Schools, and whilst quite alive to the importance of the concessions then proposed, which, however, we believe that there is little probability of procuring, we still think that the Church must prepare her mind for supporting her Schools through her own resources. She has to support her Clergy as it is, and she must make up her mind to educate her children at her own expense. It is the inevitable consequence of being a minority in the country that, however it may be disguised, any system of education compromising the religious question must inevitably Presbyterianise our Schools, and if we are to pay for separate Schools, we must at any rate take care that they do not hoist a neutral flag. The compromise is better than nothing, but let it not be in any way adopted as a general system for our Church. The grants made by Government are not so large as to find us *ad æternum*, and those grants made in the past were made on conditions to which the Government is bound to adhere unless they violate a sacred pledge.

The education of our children is, it is to be remembered, the first principle of the Church; and we might as well think of hoisting a neutral flag in the pulpit as in the school. If we are to teach Presbyterianism to our children, we are bound logically to teach it to ourselves. The casuistry refutes itself by its own subtilty. It is even more necessary to keep the Schools intact than the pulpit. We are quite enough Presbyterianised as it is without having a further shove down the hill. There is no concealing

that the ardent desire to effect an union with the Presbyterians is blinding the Bishop of St. Andrews to a
compromise, which may ultimately imperil the highest
interests of the Church ; and warmly as we have all
along sympathized in his unceasing efforts to effect a
compromise between the two systems, the more are
we convinced that any compromise that may be made
will be at the expense of the Church.   It seems improbable upon the face of it that Presbytery will
reverse its whole history.   The various charges of the
Bishop of St. Andrews are invaluable as polemical
treatises, as expository of the differences between us
and Presbytery, but furnish no basis for compromise,
unless Presbytery virtually reverses its whole principles.   The education question must then be looked
in the face.   We can have no compromise as to the
teaching of our children.   Paying for education for
the whole country is a question apart.   The compromise proposed by the Bishop of St. Andrews and the
Primus is valuable where our Church cannot support
a School of its own ; it is valuable in so far that Presbytery is not to be taught by the bayonet, but we can
regard it as a compromise in no way satisfactory to
the Church. It is true that it breaks up the sectarianism of the Parish Schools, and the general sectarianism
of the other Schools in Scotland, for at present, thank
God, they are all sectarian nearly to a man ; but to
my mind it is far preferable that the denominational

principle be preserved in its integrity, in so far that parents know what they are doing when they send their children to a school where definite principles are taught, rather than to a school where you are dependant upon the competition of the sects. A Presbyterian master is not likely to imbue children with Church principles. The petitions then that may be presented to Parliament must vary with the incidents of the situation. If we cannot retain the denominational theory, we at any rate must agitate for the compromise of a mixed education in Schools in future to be established. The present charters are binding between both parties, and the Church must not be sacrificed without a struggle ; but the main matter we have to deal with is admitting of no compromise as to the necessity of maintaining the *bona fide* Schools of the Church wherever it can be done. Our Schools have already been associated with social advantages to which all other Schools in the country are strangers, and it will be a reactionary step of the most deplorable kind, to sacrifice these Schools in hopes of getting something from Parliament that will be better. No greater delusion can be inculcated on the public mind. Any change will be for the worse. We must make the best of it, but still let us keep what we have got. Let us also not be blind to the effect of any bill for leaving open and confused the religious teaching of the children. The whole character of public thought in Scotland is provisional and sceptical. I for one cannot but look with alarm upon a scheme of education which is what is called non-sectarian. The Shorter Catechism is at any rate the formula accepted by the prepondering body of the Sects. The removing this landmark which has so long, however wrongly, guided the people, appears to me a dangerous step until we are prepared to put up something else ; and so I trust the Church will not give up her present vantage ground so long as there is a chance of maintaining it. Our children are doubtless entitled to every protection in the Schools they attend out of our jurisdiction. But it would be infinitely preferable that they should be under our control, than under a divided government with no definite principles. The Church, we trust then, will in no way resile from her position as teacher of the children. The giving up her children to facilitate a hollow compromise with the Presbyterians would be a policy at once suicidal and unjustifiable. I am fully alive to the importance of a connection with the state upon the matter of education, and even upon other matters, but experience is shewing everywhere that the state is becoming more and more hostile to all the best interests of the Church. I view with great suspicion any movement of the state which interferes with or regulates religious teaching. The Church in the main regulates her own affairs the best, and I am not prepared, because it is popular, to go in for a surrender of the vantage ground our Church has occupied, viz., that she, in the management of her Schools, is free to act in the matter of teaching as she deems most expedient. In the case of the sister Church of England, the position is altogether different. She commands a great moral influence over England, and the claims of her children are not likely to be neglected, whereas, we who occupy the position of a feeble minority in the country, are on a different platform altogether. We are struggling for our existence as a Church. We, who form a large proportion of the wealth of the country, are to be called upon to pay for Schools whose religious teaching we cannot approve of. We fully admit the obligation, for many of us have voluntarily done so without any enforcement from the State; but in going in for a more general system, it is clearly unjust to expect that we are to throw over our Schools altogether, and embark upon another scheme which is a mere "nebula" of the future. It is quite ridiculous to suppose that all our past sacrifices are to be forgotten, and that these Schools are to have a Presbyterian appendage tacked on to them. Our Schools are either Church Schools or they are not. The Schools of the future can be upon any principle you like, but it is quite another thing to say they are to be extinguished altogether. The danger of the whole movement is that it is a

downward one. We have quite enough of "Protes-
tantism" as it is called, without having more of it, for
the whole tendency of the bare Protestant principle is
in reality to believe in nothing. The whole creed of
Scotland is undergoing a radical change, and as re-
gards her Schools or any other of her public institu-
tions, it must be regarded as provisional. The
continuous movement of public thought renders all
dogmatic teaching more and more difficult. Whilst
our Church professes little or no sympathy with the
religious teaching of the sects, it is quite another thing
to say that she will have any hand in directly or indi-
rectly undermining their dogmatic teaching. However imperfect their form of Christianity is, it still is a
system which has constituted much of the social and
religious life of the country, and in sanctioning any
system of education, the maintenance, in some form or
other, of the great elements of Christianity, seems to
us essential to the whole position of our Church; for
the Church naturally sympathises with any form of
religion which recognises Christianity at all. Besides,
in the matter of the sects, she has a clear interest in
not disturbing the religious convictions of any of the
members of those religious bodies until they are prepared to receive something better or higher.

Through whatever light then the movement may
be viewed, we can detect nothing but grave evil to the
best interests of Scotland, for we perceive nothing in

the present phase of thought but what tends to subvert
and unsettle.   In deposing a dogma, we are substitut-
ing nothing.   I hold then, that the eyes of the
the whole Church will attentively be directed towards
the present aspect of affairs, and that she will in no
way diverge from her past policy.   Any retrogression
will only cause her great injury.   She cannot resile
from her present position without a forfeiture of the
confidence of the country, and getting in lieu thereof
a parasite popularity.   Any retrogression now in the
face of the attacks levelled at her upon all sides, would
only eventuate in a loss of her Schools altogether—a
confiscation of a property acquired after so much toil
—after so much obloquy and misrepresentation.   The
Church however cannot now recede even if she wished.
The loss of her present Schools would only be followed
by the erection of fresh ones, free from the meddling
of the state and the intrigues of governments.   Our
Church has never thriven under the sunshine of State
Patronage.   She requires no Privy Council to teach
her her creed.   She needs no Privy Council to educate
her children.   She has thriven only when she depended
upon herself.   If she be but true to herself, the teaching
of her children is safe.   If she depend upon an Act of
Parliament, she will trust in a broken reed.   But at the
same time let her use all constitutional means to gain
her just rights.   Let her struggle, first, for the maintenance of her existing Schools as they are, as based

upon a distinct agreement with the State; secondly, let her endeavour, if not able to start Church Schools in future, to establish such a system as will maintain intact the great primary truths of Christianity. This is the least she can accept from the State without abandoning her whole position as Teacher of the People. One point must ever be kept in view, that whatever concessions are made the Church must be the loser. So long as the State supplemented her efforts to educate her own children in the principles of her faith, the alliance with the State was defensible and salutary, but the moment the State secedes from the original contract, and plunges into the vortex of an indefinite Christianity, the position is reversed. The Church is necessarily repelled within herself, and she must necessarily depend upon herself in the education of her children. She cannot withdraw from this engagement without forfeiting all the duties of a spiritual mother. She forfeits the blessing of God in her various enterprises. She surrenders the vantage ground she at present possesses over every other denomination of Christians in Scotland. It is in the very nature of things, that when we are possessed of great temporal and spiritual advantages we value them little. We will bitterly regret their loss should we be deprived of them; so let us beware lest we, at a period of great progress and great revival, surrender the fortress, hitherto impregnable, to the foe. No increase of character—no missions—no zeal can make up for the loss of the godly teaching of the young. It is the first clause in our Church's Charter, which she has not the power, even if she willed it, to resign. There can be no tampering with this primary truth. No matter how it may be disguised, this has been the main object of all attempted legislation hitherto—under the guise of of non-sectarianism, laying the country prostrate at the feet of Presbyterianism. The Church has been roused from her sleep. She has realised the danger of her position. Let her adhere to the course she entered upon last session. Let there be one flag—not half a dozen. Let us present an united front to the enemy, and that flag have as its motto, " No Surrender." If we are to have Presbyterian Schools, let us have them openly, not under a semi-church compromise. Such appears to me the true policy of the Church in a great emergency, bearing always in mind that, whatever be the legislation, she can suffer nothing but damage. Whilst she sees inevitably the mischief which must be the result of this prospective legislation, let her gird herself to meet it. It is a matter in which all are concerned. It is essentially a layman's question, and it is by laymen the question must be taken up and dealt with, for it concerns their dearest interests as parents and citizens. If they will be but united, and not be led away by specious compromises, what remains to them will be insured ; if they adopt the downward course, and be misled by the allurements of empty popularity, they will deservedly forfeit all those advantages which they at present possess as a branch of the Church of Christ.

HUGH SCOTT,

OF GALA.

November, 1871.

By the same Author.

THE POSITION OF THE LAITY

IN THE

SCOTTISH EPISCOPAL CHURCH.

Nos. 1, 2, 3, 4, 5, 6, and 7.

PRICE 3d. EACH.

THE

FINANCIAL PROSPECTS

OF THE

Scottish Episcopal Church.

Nos. 1, 2, 3, 4, and 5.

PRICE 3d. EACH.

THE SCHOOLS

OF THE

SCOTTISH EPISCOPAL CHURCH.

Nos. 1 and 2.

PRICE 3d. EACH.

ABERDEEN: A. BROWN & CO.

THE SCHOOLS

OF THE

Scottish Episcopal Church.

No. IV.

ABERDEEN: A. BROWN & CO.

EDINBURGH: R. GRANT & SON. LONDON: LONGMAN & CO.

1872.

ABERDEEN,
PRINTED BY ARTHUR KING AND COMPANY, STEAM PRINTERS AND STEREOTYPERS
CLARK'S COURT, TOP OF BROAD STREET.

THE SCHOOLS

OF THE

SCOTTISH EPISCOPAL CHURCH.

No. IV.

THE Education Bill to be brought in by the Lord Advocate being the same as last year, leaves the Church free to determine upon the line of policy she will adopt; and to my mind, there is but one line open to her, and upon this line all the energies of churchmen should be concentrated. It has been ascertained that 85 per cent. of Scotland, more or less, belong to the Presbyterian system, and the question which Parliament has to decide is how to deal with the remaining 15. When the whole country is to be rated, it is clear that minorities are entitled to protection. It is specially so when this minority forms a large proportion of the property to be taxed for the benefit of the 85 per cent. The 15 per cent. are quite as much entitled to have religious education as the remaining 85. We are dismissing the notion of secular education as quite out of the question, as repugnant to the moral sense of the country. The Schools at present known as Church Schools, are clearly to be maintained intact. What we have to do with is the schools for the future. In this it is very clear that the 85 per cent. will take very good care that Presbyterian education shall be the rule of the School; and this we must take care must be restricted by a conscience clause. Such is evidently the policy of the Church, and to this policy she must adhere. We may calculate upon the support of our English confederates. Petitions must be presented to Parliament supporting this policy, and the Church, we entertain little doubt, will attain the object she has at heart. What I confess appeared to me to be most satisfactory during the agitation of last year, was the interest churchmen took in the matter of the Schools. We have been so often assured that the day of Church Schools had gone by—that churchmen generally considered that having any Church Schools at all was a mistake, that I myself was carried away by the confident assertions that were made thereon. The question of the Equal Dividend has settled this matter, for when an attempt was made to mix up that question with the doing away of Schools, the indignant protest of the whole Church was immediately made against so suicidal a policy. Then again, the warm interest which the Church manifested, under the leadership of the Primus, in the Education Bill, has effectively refuted the notion that the Church was disposed to give up the schools. The same warm and intelligent interest that was taken last year in the Education question will be renewed this year, we have every reason for confidently hoping. But without wishing in any way to discourage that interest, what I confess I most confidently look to, is the maintenance of the Schools through the resources of the Church herself. It will be matter of great consequence to agitate for a conscience clause, enabling the Church to start future schools, in which the denominational theory is adhered to. But it is specially important that the Church should depend more upon herself than upon any State aid. The maintenance of the Schools must necessariiy constitute the very life of the Church; and we trust that the appeal to the Church upon the matter of the education of her children will meet with as warm and successful a response as upon the matter of the Equal Dividend: The analogous instance of the Free Kirk proves that the Schools have in no way interfered with the Stipends' question, for the Schools really are the nurseries of the Church—they impart a spiritual influence to all round. Without casting any reflection upon those churches unable to support schools, there can be no doubt that the vacuum paralyzes the onward movement of the Church—

that the absence of the School paralyzes the interest felt
by Churchmen in the matters of the Church. Hence,
it is specially important that not only should the present
Schools be maintained, but that every effort should be
made to start Schools everywhere, and that the feeling
should be sedulously inculcated, that a School is essential to the proper working of the Church. We trust
that clergymen will specially impress this important
ruth in the pulpit and elsewhere. The appeal last year
was not satisfactory, for the Schools' question had been
very much lost sight of in the parliamentary contest and
in the agitation of the Stipends' question. It was in no
way representative of the feeling of the Church. It will
be, in fact, of great importance if we ignore the Education Bill altogether, for at the best the education of
our children, in a Presbyterian School, under the protection of a conscience clause, offers but small comfort.
The 15 per cent., of which we form, after all, a fraction,
have but small chance of a right education; and it
would be infinitely preferable to support a school of
our own independently. Nothing we can get from
the State can be satisfactory, in fact, unless our
Schools be maintained in their integrity. We are
not sorry that the Education question is thus brought
before us, for it teaches us how the matter really stands.
It points out the danger really impending over us, and,
we trust, will nerve us for the struggle we must engage

in; this, too, in the height of our prosperity, when we are carrying with us so much of the public feeling of the country. The 85 per cent. belonging to Presbyterians is more ostensible than real. It belongs to Presbytery very much, because it is externally associated with Presbytery. It is very much like saying that a man belongs to the establishment, because he does not belong to a voluntary body. If we analyse the voluntary bodies themselves, it is questionable how far a belief in Presbytery forms a *bona fide* part of their system. It is believed in because it is a traditional creed. There is indeed a large class who believe in Presbytery, I grant, and whose belief is *bona fide*, but there is a still larger class who are at present in a transition state. We are not anxious that in consequence there should be any suspension of the dogmatic teaching, nor are we anxious to contribute to the unsettlement; all that we are anxious for is, that the 85 per cent., which we regard as a mere nominal figure, should not domineer over the country, and still more do we object to a transition theology or a compromised Christianity. We are anxious that the dogmatic teaching of all the creeds should be retained in its integrity, always under the protection of a conscience clause. The main duty of the Church in the meantime is to retain the teaching of her children in her own hands so far as possible, to propagate her schools through the breadth and length of the country, and to maintain her training institution. The question of the Education Bill is, so far as the Church is concerned, of secondary importance. There is a danger of doing a deal of mischief. There is little probability of its doing us much good. So long as the Church be true to herself in the matter of the Schools, she is bound to provide against unjust aggression, and to protect herself from a practical plunder of her property; whilst bound to guard her future interests so far as possible, she need not fear much any Education Bill. It shows true weakness when a Church depends upon an Act of Parliament. The whole history of our Church is a living testimony against dependence on the secular arm. So long as the Church fulfils her clear duty, she will have the protection and blessing of God. When she looks for support elsewhere, she falters in her first love. The Church must ever depend upon her spiritual power and her spiritual development. Strip her of these, and you leave her prostrate at the feet of the world. The world respects her most when she cares least about it. The Schools' question then forms the primary question of the Church, for it concerns her whole spiritual existence as a Church of Christ. The revival of her Schools was the initiatory symptom of her revival as a Church. By the admission of the Presbyterians themselves, they have been beneficial to the whole community. Their maintenance should strain our financial energies, for should we ever realize a £200 minimum for our clergy—an event little likely of accomplishment in a Church spiritually dead—of what advantage would it be, did it paralyze and eat up the spiritual life of a part of the body of Christ? Would it not be a stain upon the priesthood to be the priesthood of a Church spiritually dead? We trust then that Churchmen will not look upon the Schools' question as one that may or may not be taken up at random. It concerns the first principles of the Catholic Church. It is one of the tests of a falling or standing Church. In the present transitional phase of religious thought in Scotland, it is specially important that we should retain in its integrity the dogmatic teaching of the Church in all the departments of the Church's machinery, that we should present a firm and consistent attitude before the country, so that he who runs may read. No vacillating policy, no infirmity of purpose, no timid intriguing with statesmen, should mark the track of our Church. There can be but one line for the Church to take ; and that is to maintain and propagate her Schools, to retain a firm hold over the teaching of her young. Should she recede from this position, she will sink lower than she ever did, even in the dreary days of the First Charles, for she will neglect her first duty as a Spiritual Mother.

HUGH SCOTT,
OF GALA.

CANNES, *February,* 1872.

By the same Author.

THE POSITION OF THE LAITY
IN THE
SCOTTISH EPISCOPAL CHURCH.
Nos. 1, 2, 3, 4, 5, 6, and 7.—*Price* 3D. *each.*

THE FINANCIAL PROSPECTS
OF THE
SCOTTISH EPISCOPAL CHURCH.
Nos. 1, 2, 3, 4, and 5.—*Price* 3D. *each.*

THE SCHOOLS
OF THE
SCOTTISH EPISCOPAL CHURCH.
Nos. 1, 2, and 3.—*Price* 3D. *each.*

THE COMING GENERAL SYNOD
OF THE
SCOTTISH EPISCOPAL CHURCH.
No. 1.—*Price* 2D.   No. 2.—*Price* 3D.

ABERDEEN: A. BROWN & CO.

www.ingramcontent.com/pod-product-compliance
Lightning Source LLC
Chambersburg PA
CBHW081526040426
42447CB00013B/3355